**These poems are of life and thoughts.
In the depths of one's soul exist a world,
a world that may never be explored.
I have scratched the fringes of my world
and it's filled with rainbows.
Come let's enjoy it together.
They shine brighter when they shine
for others.**

Joseph A. Bain

Editor: Jacqueline Bain

Cover Design by Winston Berrotte
Researcher: Joseph Bain Jr.

Published by Joseph A. Bain
For further information:
P.O. Box 47039
300 Borough Dr.
Scarborough Ontario
Canada
M1P-4Z7

e-mail: jbwrite@msn.com
ISBN 0-9680847-0-2
Published in Canada

MEET THE AUTHOR

I am Joseph Bain, born in Grenada, West Indies. I was born and raised in the near suburbs of St. Georges the capital in a tiny village by the sea called Fontenoy. My parents were church going folks. My father worked for the Health Department, a job that took him traveling throughout the island as he visited various job sites he managed. My mother stayed home to manage the business and when I think of it today, I wonder how she did it all. There was the little shop she tended all day and still found time for the cooking and house cleaning. She was assisted by some paid help with the washing and gardening such as tilling and the reaping of the crops which was more than her five boys and one girl could handle. If my father was not back home from work at the expected time, she would have to check the catch of the day with the fishermen who fished in our boats.

The children had the animals to tend to. The cows had to be milked and looked after before going off to school, but at nine o'clock we had to be at the door of the school with no excuses. I was schooled at St. Georges Anglican School, a name which is rarely used on the island to describe schools which are usually christened by the names of their principals. In other words, if I was to tell this to someone from Grenada, I will tell them that I went to Mr. Hinds' School. Mr. Hinds was that unforgettable principal who made English literature so very fascinating to me.

I grew closer to my mother as I grew older and we spent more time speaking of things from the heart. Through all of her busy days she still found time to listen to me. When the subject matter was too much for her, she would consult with my father who always seemed to have the answers.

Therefore, one could rightfully say that I was rounded on all sides so to speak.

I came to Canada in 1969 and one year thereafter I married my native sweetheart, but there was another love in my life that would not stop haunting me and that was literature. I felt that irresistible need to explore my interest for the written word. I therefore did correspondence courses for a short while. My work was highly credited but unfortunately I terminated it because there were other job related courses which needed to be completed.

Approximately seventeen years later when I found myself back in the classroom nourishing that immortal word and loving it. When I thought I was comfortable with my writing skills I started writing a book. I wrote for approximately five years before destroying it, dissatisfied with the caliber of my work. I did not allow myself to be hindered by that, instead I persevered onward with further studies until I found the author in me. During a second attempt at the said book, I stumbled upon a character who loved poetry. Each time I slipped into that character it felt like slipping on an old pair of comfortable shoes. I was swept away writing these poems.

My priest gave me permission to deliver a Sunday sermon which I ended with one of my poems. That was the beginning of my public poetry reading exposure. From then onward I have read my poems throughout the city of Toronto. At Parkdale Library for Black History Month, at Burke's for Kwanzaa , at church functions with audiences of up to four hundred plus. One of my most cherished readings was at a luncheon at the Howard Johnson Hotel for the Prime Minister of Grenada, Carriacou and Petit Martinique, Dr. Keith Mitchell and an audience of five hundred. I also appeared on a radio show which featured my poetry. That experience along with the encouragement tied the knot and made me realize that I had to put more of myself into the writing of my poetry.

A note to students in the art of poetry, don't expect to get the full meaning or impact of the poems in one reading. My poetic language is unique and my experiences are different

from yours. Look for the thought of the poems within your own emotions.

Not for one minute have I regretted coming to this beautiful land called Canada or making it my adopted home. My dreams came true, all my dreams laden with the finest harvest. I take my hat off and say, "To Canada, with love".

I thank my beautiful wife Ann who is the source and strength , and after 26 loving years of marriage, we still hug each other while strolling in the mall. Special thanks to my son Joseph Jr. He is a special person who warms my heart and the hearts of all those he meets along the way. My daughter Jacqueline is the boss who occupies that tender place within my heart where only a daughter is allowed. I hope and pray I can give more of my service to the work of God through the Anglican Church.

In all my future endeavors I hope I can be of service to the people of Grenada and of Canada.

You can find me among the little people. I cheer for the runners who come from behind to finally win the race.

ACKNOWLEDGEMENTS

I will first thank God who has given me this gift. Special thanks to my wife Ann who believes in me and supports me most kindly along the way. My children Joseph Jr. and Jacqueline who I am particularly grateful to for their contribution over the years.

Special thanks to my Priest, Rev. Elizabeth Hardy for her prayers and continuous support. I also gratefully acknowledge the valuable advice and encouragement of the following families; Stanley Munroe and family, Lynell Nolan and family, David Davis and family and last but not least, Donny Israel and family.

For the teacher who heard me read my first poem publicly and made me realize that I have a gift of value that should not die but should be pursued. I cannot thank you enough, my greatest appreciation to you Mrs. Mildred Lane-Miller.

To all my brothers and sisters in my church, St. Michael the Archangel Anglican Church, let me say I love you, you were always there for me with your prayers and giving me opportunities to express my art. I thank you.

Thanks to the youth in my church school for their questions that sent me searching my soul and when I saw the answers through their eyes it brought grace to the pages of my work.

I also gratefully acknowledge all of my relatives and friends both here in Canada and in Grenada. Your optimism for me powered me onward.

I will like to thank the friends I have not yet met, it will be my greatest pleasure meeting you.

CONTENTS

I dedicate this book in loving memory of my parents

Ivan and Louisa Bain.

I AM, WE ARE THE FATHERS

Creation has shaped me with that roar,
With armored soul
I must be strong.
But my roar can be as soft as a hush,
That makes them hush.

The lead I must take even when my foundation
shakes in storms of disbelief.
Beneath this rock cradles a spring of care,
It's okay to flow my tears.

I must be on the tips of their tongues.
They must touch me for that final say.
I must be there to catch that ball,
To break their fall.
I am the father.

The road of our name must not be strewn
with debris of disgrace.
Blameth not us.
Let the suit of blame be worn by the designer,
We are not the fit.

Guide the children.
We must take them from fledglings to wings that
soar o'er the highest star,
That's who they are.

God's strength is in you, even in your graying few.
We were given the torch to light the way
not burn the tracks.
At the end, the end of the day,
We must be proud to say,
I am, we are the fathers.

It's written across the sky to
my beloved wife with all my love.

MY LOVE

These hearts entwined and bind with
strings of sweetness yet.
For sweet I know, when bitterness as from
the earth it grows.
We blaze like streams, into streams of
fragrance buried in the warmth of
flickering embers.

So few men know when upon moistened
fields to grow,
Yet fall like leaves on autumn nights
where fallen colours lay, in trampled
promises of yesterday.

To know you is to ask myself,
Who chose this path to meet?
Was it destiny? Same destiny of which I
heard from sad fallen men.
But when the day is noonday bright,
Why ask myself where is the darken night.

Those fallen men just broke their stride,
To tarnish names of humble bride.
Oh no, not I, I'll exhault you dear if need be,
And raise myself I will, to touch the summit of
my soul, within your loving thrill.
I love you, and I love you.

This poem was written to commemorate my twenty five years of service as a staff member of The Physical Plant Services of The Wellesley Hospital.

It illustrates some vivid images and recollections of my experience.

WHAT SONG DO YOU SING IN THE EVENING

It's vivid, but sometimes so vague.
As carpet colours change, enhancing blushing walls,
And offices appear where once was bare,
With dancing keyboards, while fleeting images
cross square coloured screens.

Corridors of ease stretch endlessly now,
So my aching feet select those cushioned tiles.
Faces in elevators all seem replaced,
My name they knoweth not, nor my face.

Let's talk of those days when happiness
greeted you at the door
like parents who cared for each other we were,
With shoulders there,
So tears from painful heads never flowed.

Youths with quickening stride
shake their heads as they go by.
To them,
Ancient history whose pages seem too gloom,
Like them I was, not long ago
drumming the night long with my tune.

But time smiles, into its archives as it stores,
Recurring lives, not memoirs, names may never show.
Just cherish the Wellesley faces and let them be
each with its sweet differences, just like you or me.
Within those walls God's peace I did explore,
You add that colour to my rainbow
not just a revolving door.

A BLESSING IN GIVING

And with this breath, as to breathing I
hold so fast.
As life's sweetness rests upon my tongue.
But not my soul, oh soul I pledge to thee.
Alas, my God alas.

If hoarding diamonds is a poor man's dream,
Then I'll never sleep beneath that sky.
Where smiles are linked but links retrieve,
Just accept, so I can thank thee for my smile.

Moreover and then over again,
I clasp my mind to someone's dream.
And dream they will for nature's sake,
That paradise's comfort waking takes.

For here I give not rose nor wine,
For such delight I haveth not,
Just accept this morsel, so my heart can smile.
To have and not give, I'd rather not.

STILL WATERS

The wind that wrote upon my mind,
As now I dare see years of intricate designs
lick the cool horizons with dancing flames
upon its tongue.
Bridges that hugged us within its palms,
Helplessly lay cross legged submerged
within the river beds.

Sacred buildings where sacrifices aired the
disturbances of our souls,
Now tarnish the layers of enemies boots,
While bloated carcasses of our children
tattoo the braided highways,
And vultures expose their virgin bones
insulting the ancient sun.

Now with that demolishing power
we camped under the fragments across
the broken table,
And listened for that golden preciousness
to drench the desert for our forgotten souls.
Peace.

Is there no peace? Only headlines.
Headlines that miss the kiss of lullabies
as we usher our babies into a night where
hope lives in the morrow.

Is there no peace? Then what a vainless
search I do endure. When in its absence
turmoil engulfs my soul.
And I sigh,
With regrets of the blindness that will
lead us into oblivion.

THE FACE OF TRUTH I DID SEE MOMENTARILY

There was a voice, as clear as crystals fair,
No haste or time, or human's rhyme.
But stood the clouds away,
Not venture near its glitter or
darken its untimely flicker,
But it was not yet my time.

Its gender hid beneath a shawl of
angels colours,
Where streams of light, like rivers that
quenches earth's thirst.
Deep streams that boast they sprang
from heavenly source.

It's hair hanged bright, like a thousand
candles on a darkened night,
And upon the shawl it made its bed.

Mine eyes knew it fought a loss,
Then looked away,
And mounted tall my hair on edge as
though each to be counted.

That voice fearlessly charged
with few in it's ranks
with equal power to match,
And there stood spineless lies among
the mortals, With absent brag beneath
surrender's flag.

Then call the mortals did to join their foe,
To band the ranks of truth,
And stood they did astute.
But only those that crossed the river
wore the shawl of truth.
But it was not yet my time.

THE LOVER IN YOUR DREAMS

You go on hurrying your days
like most of us do,
Filling them with incomplete
yesterdays, yes you do.
Then tumbling into that irresistible
foliage that recharges your good
morning as your eyelids invite the night.

With her breathless sounds, she whispers
that which only you can tell,
And wonder unfolds before you
with romantic promises so swell.

Then unto the dark side of the moon
where faces are lit by your thoughts.
With eyes not squinting with surprise
in that huggable land that's not.

You kiss, kisses of laughter
while you turn pages of lovers games.
That's where destiny is revealed,
But a place that holds no blame.

Then with your strength replenish.
You are the only one who knows.
No jealous questions to answer
of your lover in repose.
Because waking, is not taking any guilt,
For the lover in your dreams.

Look into the eyes of your soul , feel its rhythm.
Your emotions rhythm where you have full control.
It's in the rhythm of your skin.
This is the rhythm of mine.

IN THE RHYTHM OF MY SKIN

Where is my gold, where is my gold
that creation has placed beneath my feet?
I go on thanking the sun.
Where is my Eden
where the animals run so free?

Did he ask for me, that giraffe
that wakes the monkeys way up in
the trees?
Just to hear me laugh my childish
laugh in a thousand keys.

Has my mother's hair turned to the colour
of her captors face?
Was her sash wide enough to support
her sobbing waist?
How many moons did she dance the
grieving dance before it rained?

Did my father with his spear chase bullets
thinking they were evil spirits?

Her feet never honored this land,
My dear sister I know so well.
She makes peace among the seas
just like she did with my brother and me.

They say she sang the elephant song,
The song the elephants sing when they
are carried by the wind to that place
where the road ends and their bones begin.

For me, I soar with the eagles as
they sleep on their wings,
And find comfort with my God who
lives within,
And expresses himself
in the rhythm of my skin.

WIND OF NOTHINGNESS
DEATH

Let the flutist tune the wind
that grows out of the south.
It's that same wind you know
that will some day on us round about.
Death.

You boldly seize a place,
Oh wind of nothingness.
And stand next to names of angels
on stones of tombs and crypts.

Let's celebrate life,
Let champagne numb our minds.
Dust that aging wine,
Let's toast to life here, here!
To the living.

If I mourn then I celebrate a void,
How do you rate a void?

Think of a place where they
dance on graves.
Where they insult that resident of hell
with no face unless given.
Let us live among the living
and their passing we won't tell.

Your road must be spring in every root
where they touch the meaning of your name
on innocent heads o'er holy fountain.
And tell their friends in honest truth
he will be just like you, yes, she will
be just like you.

Now bow your faceless head in shame
you who make the mind forget.
When life is sweet, it's incomplete
if not followed by our death.

So be that flutist, tune that wind
of life that tastes so well,
And live, find your true purpose in life,
And live that life to its fullest.

LITTLE BROWN DOVE

Preserve your foremost compass
like a folded sail on a schooners deck.
Your nest is cluttered with stored remains
and your purpose well met.

Do you know a place
where the rain drops are heated
in their chase?
Not drifting in frozen floes.

Where little boys with crooked
slingshots are all you have to fear,
And through the thickets and the groves
blows the ripening tropical air.

Where good morning cannot be
misunderstood. The sun rises
bearing it's gifts and prizes.
And they listen to the rooster as it
chases the night, in the morning.

When the calm comes
don't fly due south.
I need your company in my illusion
of wealth and promise.
Or is it in my sandy ceiling here as I gaze
on this cold Saturday morning haze?

IN SOLITUDE

In solitude the sand-is golden
and molded into symbols of truth.
If unseen through the ripples
of your thoughts you accept
what the glaring surface says,
And wonder how did the weeping willow
grow so majestic in its tears.

Bathe your face. I say bathe your face
like a thousand faces in the
dim morning light.
Now step where it's bright.
Trash the dark side of that mountain
with a prayer.

Wisdom awaits you there.
Full trains on cotton tracks,
Humble wisdom hibernating
like a virgins wish.

You wonder why you are there.
It's just for a visit.
You see, the weakest link must exert
the most of its strength,
It's purpose there to meet,
Or all stare into the eyes of defeat.
In solitude.

A HUG, JUST A HUG

You are the medicine,
A dose that never overdoses.
Just a hug.
Silent healing that hangs at your side
filling warm pockets
from shoulder sockets.
They must be sewn.

Sew that love portion, let it grow.
When words retrieve from whence
they came, and all seems vain,
Split that air.
That bright ray for tomorrow that's
comfortable clouded in darkness,
Bring sunshine there.

Solid foundation you'll add to a
dream. Drape your arms around that
special someone.
Decorate their day like an artist's mind.
It is easier than it seems.

Then say bygosh, I did it.
See those optimistic smiles you
just stole from the moon.
They are playing your tune,
Because you are the medicine
with just a hug.

TORONTO'S WEATHER

In Toronto you say,
May thaw may not be thawing.
Mailcarriers footprints still
trail from your door.
But the sun never slants in disgust
in the heated month of August.

The January sky kisses the frozen
waterfront, that's rich in artist's rhymes.
And summer dresses leap from Paris designs
to unlatch greenhouses anxious wait.

The magic that touches all seasons four,
This fair city has compressed into two.
From ski slopes to baseball diamonds,
From snowballs to flowering baby's breath.
The whitest white and the greenest green,
That is Toronto through and through.

Don't dress for the weather, it dresses you.
It keeps conversations alive.
An excuse for cheaters, the flame for lovers.
Amazing extremes where the city thrives.

I will sing of the season we met.
It will be one or the other.
Will it be the happy geese or the
frozen ghost of the golfer?
That is Toronto's weather.

I AM PEACE

I looseth not a war I ever waged,
You know my face rage,
You know my face.
It's the only face you fear
and fear you must, for Heaven's sake.

You clench your fists but my
laughter was so loud, then I hugged
my enemies and stood so proud.
I am peace.

Why crush flesh and bones that weren't
made for crushing?
What can dust to dust convey,
When out of tranquil souls I forever flow
to moisten tomorrow's happy day.
I am peace.

Forsake me not for comforts sake,
For comfort dwells but within a dream.
With empty skies, shoreless seas
rattling winter's teeth and summers so lean.
I am peace.

I am the gentle breeze that precedes
and lingers there to heal,
And heal I will in songs that stretch
from shore to shore where I live on
in chiming hearts forever more.
I am peace.

THE DANCE

The hands that beckon you unto
the swinging floor, oh I wish they
were mine.
As I stare into my suds and nod to
questions I've never heard.

His words are like velvet and as warm
as an inviting smile of innocence,
Encircled by his sneer.
You saw no one yet as his lapel
pillowed your warm breath.

Oh how I wish the music stops,
No, no let it play all night, all day,
Then hope remains on every note
and my wish they all convey.

But let my wish be a beggar's wish,
they must not come true.
See I'm on the dance floor next you.
Love songs tell my lies and fill your
every need, while my heart is crushed.
Is it love or is it greed?

Am I not a robber then
if driven by same thoughts,
Condemning men of sinful acts,
Acts I'll act if got.

THE TEST OF LOVE

Doth lying eyes twinkle like a falling star
to be concealed in hollow caverns
where echoes are lost,
Or loses its glow in disguise
ne'er heal but sly thyself like the winter's frost.

Mine eyes have fooled not self but heart.
My senseless ears your words complete.
By standards anew whose lips were soft
like snowflakes on my skin.
To conquer and defeat.

Face to face the melting of my soul,
Like glaciers in the early spring.
Where creatures stunned, their lives to give,
Their carcasses and their skin.

How dare your lies so fully clothe,
Which warm my nights where love I strode.
In moonlit lives on forbidden shores,
Sweet pain I cherish for ever more.

I LOVE THEE LORD

How then is thy silkĕn touch,
That numbs the souls of men,
Who yearn to hide deceitful hearts
for their own desires when.

Where is the source of that wind
that drives giants to their knees,
before altars far and wide,
And soothes babies as they sleep
in that innocent by and by.

There are thy words, when words are few.
That parted hindrance deep,
Or that star to follow oh Shepherd
of thy sheep.

Can I touch thee Lord? If touching is
assuring eyes.
Or should I dance among the crowd
with outstretched arms held high?
Or should I say I love thee when mortal
feelings persist?
When my love resides in faith
where men have since resisted.

Then how can I say I love thee Lord
in tongues of humble men?
And sleep, dear sleep in confidence
for answers heaven sent.
But I touch heaven when I say,
I love thee Lord.

October 19th, 1983.

A day of painful remembrance for all Grenadians.

There is a stone in my heart, which also crushes
the heels of Grenadians memories everywhere.
I am speaking of the day rage lingered over the
Hill in Paradise Land. When the darkness had
lifted with its woe and pain, and the ricocheting
echoes of screams and bullets faded. We
searched for the lost ones, which in our hearts we
knew were lost to mortality, never realizing they
were gone inconspicuously.
On this unfortunate day, a father kissed his
children goodbye as they headed off to school,
little did they did know it was their last kiss.
Someone said they were last seen on the Hill. He
goes to the Hill after searching fruitlessly elsewhere
for answers. He scratches the surface of the Hill
vainlessly day after painful day. In his heart the
only music that played, played the notes of hope
while tears of energy drained him. In his plight he speaks
to the Hill. There in the world of my poetic mind
I heard him, and these are the words I distinguished
in the pit of his tears.

THE HILL

I know you hugged the ears of innocence
from fearful seagull cries.
Never shivering at that curfew call
replacing sun filled skies.

Oh Hill that never concealed pirates
buried woes,
Those restless chests of emptiness
which purchased human souls.
You give yourself to all but seek
comfort on the bosom of the waves,
To hush your groaning streams with
its squalls.

You never crave to be history's page
with roots so covered in pain,
Or display scars upon your face as
a playing field for rage.
Your flowers never sipped that cloud
to quench the seasons thirst,
But withered in gun powdered storm
of faces with no remorse.

So let the moon's breath part your branches.
That's when my children
come out to play, with your discarded
leaves, warm their feet where so ever
they may lay.
Their broken pencils I'll place like candles,
Their guide so let it be.
And when the howling turns to wagging,
I'll rest my weary feet, that's when, you'll see.

THE BACHELOR

Home is where the heart is
so they say.
My heart wonders from day to day,
Falling in and out of my door
my welcoming mats reach up to
greet me once more.
Gone is that thrill in my Monday
morning smile, that made my living
stand on edge.
Now on the edge of life I stand
holding no one's hand but mine.

I stumble up Saturday night stairs
shaking the brew in my graying few,
And listen to my squeaking hinge complain,
"Lonely highway, one man one way.
Bosom beauties have disappeared like
their bosoms did."

Let me take my voice and mix it
with your matured flavored cheeks
and taste what's left of me.
Would you let me?
Would you help break that spell of
strength gone limp that now mocks
my feet supporting splint.

My space resembles only me.
It mirrors the skill I never find,
Another heart for me to bind.
Give me your soul, teach me to share
thine own sweet stillness upon my ledge,
Where stone angels caressed by thee, but
pleases me.

Then I can count lonely heart beats as
they fade, as someone closes my window shade,
Than shade myself with closing walls.

IN THE MIDST OF IT ALL THERE IS LOVE

Has your heart breathed the purest breath.
That feeling that holds you, and folds you.
Once touched by love, you ne'er forget,
Love catches one in the twinkle of an eye
Among the crowd, it feels like a
gentle breeze. Or a simple, Hi.

Sometimes its like a silence tucked beneath
the moon,
Or a song that chased the morning haze
and leaves you daylong humming its tune.

'Tis the sweet swirling of your soul,
It takes you beyond comprehension,
Away from the faces of why,
to the promises you ne'er mention.

When you are your lowest low,
Love is your highest high.
A gentle racing of your heart to one who cares
where words should not enter if
disguised as a lie.

Within one's heart glows a space,
Which reads. " Reserved for love."
Has it occupied love?
Because when you are your lowest low,
Love is your highest high.
And in the midst of it all there is love.

LOST TO A MIRROR

The diamond comes first
not the reflection of course.
The object shadow is cast
not taken to enrich that which
already is.

With a limp, your soul has surfaced
measured with a tool, spells disgrace.

Tossing, incapable of flight,
we stand with fragility
toughing our words into granite.
Words with souls that exist with
immortality.

What shape now are we as we tarry,
Looking up at shadows that move
without the sun, eluding everyone.

Or dare we ask of our lines or past.
Irrelevant, just irrelevant.
But standing there before us proud
dressed in clandish shroud,
Absorbing our light but not our word.

*My mother died suddenly at age forty eight,
and we gave her our tears on which to
sail back to Heaven.*

FRAGRANCE OF TEARS

She was the air that painted flowers
everywhere, but knew she would not see
her's bloom because angels kiss goodbye
in May,
And her roses will bloom in June.

As I rock myself on the edges,
Submerged in pledges,
You rest out of reach never out of mind,
Pleasantness you left behind.

Grasp my manly hand to cross.
Cross that cross.
Or do I embrace what leads me
through the day, and taste my
tears on pillows.

Oh dear mother, am I not weaned
from breast,
Or do I cling like vine, not making
reality mine?

Why didn't you let time complete your love?
Then I am high and I'm dry on solid ground.
Just your name and I splash, you are in
my watery eyes like a pool, not a dash.

THE DAY THE POET'S INK RAN DRY

How can your words run out?
Creator of words.
You who make them larger than themselves.
Has the wind exhausted its source?
Or love be gone, when lovers winks
light city squares.

A poet was he,
But was he not a running bird with wings
that swept the ground.
Not a soul that's crisp with tenderness
but can cut the edges of lightening
amidst the thundering sky.

Your harvest basket on its axis spins
volcanically.
Did you write your Sunday best?
Or is this your best Sunday when you don't.

Why arm yourself with words
and toss emotion to the ground.
Words speak more in fewness
than on babbling liars tongue.

The green of meadows plays in summer.
But goodbye only says the green
while perennials cuddle beneath the moons,
For kissing bouquets on homecoming queens.

Every bright tomorrow shines around
a corner, and shine it does.
Every lover has walked
the tattered streets of love.
Coins are tossed but dormantly lay subdued
to it's wish.
But coins are mere coins.

Awake and paint the world betwex
and between those lines.
Awake those feelings which are dressed
to dress lovers tender night.
Conduit of eternity, your messages are to guide.

THE CITY AWAKES

Invading beams like from unknown galaxies.
The all night deejay through the rear exits.
The street sweeper pokes his first flying page, in rage.
The night never knew the moon existed.

The sun slaps the bleak yawning cloud,
To count the skyscrapers floor starting from above.
Fifty-five solar gatherings came alive,
Fifty-four was blinded like fifty-three.
Fifty-two was dumbfounded, it's lovers still in love.
Fifty-one took a stand for a fee.

Whispers of a ray mischievously sprang ahead
to melt the heaps of dreams.
'Twas late in stride, the heated grill had already interceded.

Warm like his breath that parted the whispering wind.
He shook with a flare, that clump of rags.
Down the canopied lane,
All but two trips with his bags.

"This spot was warmed by an angel",
As he placed his world gently down.
"I'm not disturbing heaven's children."
He stumbled to the bin.
"Just to brace myself my son, for lately the mission
line stretches another yard
and all the faces seem unscared.

Nervous beads dangled down his brow
where time now like a vulture feasts.
'Til death do you part, but such a parting is death.
His only fret, the city never hugs him when it sleeps.

I followed my beam to my unknown galaxy,
Kiss the daylight on the foreheads of my name.
They lay in sweet slumber but full of life,
Now where are the rules of tomorrow's game?

SILENT ICE. THE TENOR

The crowd was on its feet, same time
shoulder to shoulder space like all
those years of antiquities and lace.
With exploding lungs that loosen the tears
of widows and their riches over the years.

He fell to his knees overcome by his song.
Bravo, bravo,
Words that disgusted his son,
Who never could have seen an act of bravery.
His sweat fogged the mirrored floor
where the curtains polished the years away.

And there catching every note in frenzy like
palms, to nourish their nightly souls,
And for that moment their husbands it seems
were not in forever land but petticoat dreams.

As they limp through their day,
This allegro brings their pains to rest.
Where the villain changes its dress.
Now the lion lay wounded, unable to soar.
His eyes curl into the lights, begging
for his roar.
That voice! King of the night has just taken flight.

Who am I if not King of the night?
Where essence of my coronations make
jealous royalty spent in vestation,
On tongues of peasants in fields I'll be,
Where libation pours from empty goblets
and chandeliers glitter they never did see.

The curtain hung its head in shameless closure,
Like silent ice of the voiceless tenor.

This poem evolved into an enlightening play, which I pray will be staged so all can enjoy it.

THE CANADIAN VISA STORY

She smiled with a bitter taste
her wish had concealed.
The boldness of the printed maple
confirmed permission to its distant land,
Yet her words disguised her aching heart,
And creases of her smile soothed ripples
over her reply.

"Oh happiness without warning,
Why depart!" Screamed a lonesome heart.
"Or why should my dance end now that
the music is finally here.
To the world I must give what I had set apart.
Go my child. I'll cherish the pain we were
severed not from the heart."

Twenty tears of dancing city lights
refuse to cast its shadows on my thoughts.
Those youthful songs that cradle the
coolness of memories past still light my
face with pride as I visit its ambitious tones.

I have learned to remain hidden within
my own words while I cry my tears back
into its fountain just like my mother did.

But I wonder, will my spirit lead them
through those tracks of spicy leaves
where the links of my name go to rest?
Or begin a new and dusty road, with flowers
resting on my breast.

Happy twenty fifth wedding anniversary
my all.
You are but the breath I breathe.

THE YEAR IS SILVER BUT YOU ARE MY GOLD

You said so few words,
but heavens gates flew open
when they touched my heart.
We melted into each others dreams
just walking hand in hand it seems.
And my guardian angel whispered,
"Till death do you part."

And we dance to the rhythm in
the evening glow with gentle
arms still encircling the early dawn.
We lit the night like it never missed the sun.
We were love, we were music, all rolled
into one.

I conquered no shores,
No fame or fortune bestowed upon me,
Yet you made me your hero but
my armor was you.
Oh angel, such an angel, what ever
did you see in me.

And we dance to the rhythm in
the evening glow with gentle
arms still encircling the early dawn.
We lit the night like it never missed the sun.
We were love, we were music, all rolled
into one.

Your reflection in this mirrored city
where we choose to roost,
Exists within your gentle shade of calmness,
A calmness that's unbreakable with fury or force.
Clinging to you is easy, you keep me on course.

And we dance to the rhythm in
the evening glow with gentle
arms still encircling the early dawn.
We lit the night like it never missed the sun.
We were love, we were music,
all rolled into one.

God's gift was two, that cute little girl
resembles you.
And my son, ha ha, is like my
youthful mirror.

With never ending love, shining on us
from above because what God has joined
together, let no one put asunder.

And we dance to the rhythm now
soft and slow, while our hearts take
the lead within us.
Not longer, just sweeter we circled
the floor,
In the warmth of each others feet
beneath us.

FRIENDSHIP

Rest your heavy heart in mine,
I'll cushion that space.
Those waves of thundering beats
displaced as you toss and turn,
Flax and burn.
I will for thee an oasis be.

Can I walk away when my heart will
stay where footsteps trod upon my soul,
Locked in secret dungeons that
comforts pain,
With shallow smile, where lost seems gain.

Not for your love but beloved oh dear,
As seasons greet the distant sun.
Hug me, kiss my cheek,
Disturb the secrecy within the deep.
Nothing I ask in return,
Just half your load that makes you
weak makes you feel it's meant for you
and you alone.
It's not dear friend, it's not.
Trust this one for myself I speak.

This friendship we share not like
boastful love built on pyramids of ease,
Where artists nights drape priceless walls
to cage roaming footsteps of deceit.

We caught the softest falling snow,
Painted structures built on trust.
Elevate your feet, close your eyes,
In my leaving I'll put out the light.

DANCE TO DEATH A CAPTIVE OF RAGE

Awake me, please awake me
from this slumber that paralyses
my soul.
Strength, oh strength why has
thou deceived me.
I'm captured by these invisible chains
while vampires lick the severed
arteries of my mind.

Those parading footsteps outside my door
hurriedly carting their victims away.
How I await their halting order to
deliverance's noose that will slide
my breath away.

'Twas death, not torment that echoed
the judges gavel,
And for its everlasting honey I'll
await no more.

In the distance I hear children's laughter
while I am lost in a manhood of pain.
Creations refuse I am, with no
marking to my name.

No more chances at life I ask,
Unless taught life's expected worth.
Don't place me among powers that
overpowers power leading me to this
destruction of my soul.

You condemn me, now go forget me.
Let me be the wind that never blew.
A disturbed soul that awaits its glory,
a glory no one ever knew.

LOVE LETTERS IN THE ATTIC OF THE MIND

On wings to your windowed envied
stage bearing songs to your
window dressing,
As lines and circles fill blank pages
of silk to await it's mailing.

In lovers symphony I serenade you
with my applause,
But tomorrow's diamonds await thee.
Again I'll write into the night
where the peace of you awaits me.

Band of gold with tender noose
in his tuxedos laughter he'll be
revealing the date he met to
yesterday's smile,
He'll recite on the threshold of
your evening.

But that voiceless moon on lovers night,
In folded pages on my pillow rests,
In diaries stored in my mind
for someone not yet intended.

MY GRANDMOTHER

Once there was a rock humbly inviting
every morn on her knees,
And planting the strength of ten
thousand years into your soul,
With just one word.

Her age she never told,
But toll the church bell on the hill.
The tracks on her face were seldom
traveled by a smile but in her heart
they ran so wild.

She hums her songs bringing the
words to light only when it chips
away at her granite.

There was always space at her place
for one more.
And on her table she set a setting
for that stranger she never met.

A prophet grew on my family tree,
Anchoring hopes in my children
so deep,
Within the granite once chipped away,
And I gather them all at her humble feet.

THE PET ROCK OBSERVES

Lenses adore live colours on dying leaves.
Sand castles fall but not to the tide.
Sand storms are rooted where
once grew trees.
Side effect unknown but prescriptions
prescribe.

Playgrounds of machines you challenge
with coins, where races are won
but not shared with the breeze.
Cheered by sounds that cannot
compare to laughter of playmates
beneath those trees.

Heads of extinction, what were your
forest calls?
Are they on hunters trophies
proudly carved in?
I must age before I am scratched for
these clues.
This is the axis on which your
world spins.

Now lay me in my show box
don't ruffle my hair,
Go inherit your name.
But who will be that someone that
really cares, for pet rocks and their
little friends.

Love is fearless, no beginning or end,
But life is comforted in fear.
With ears pressed against the ground
you forget from whence you came,
And love dies so fear can live.

LOVE, LIFE AND FEAR

He felt like a minstrel
at the princess' feet.
Transported there only by his voice,
Never to see her dawning desire,
Their worlds were in full retreat.
Dashing garments surround her,
Colourful stench of arrogance in disguise.
Yet gently building the framework of her mind,
So close but searching yet to find,
'Tis this discorded one,
Lamed like distant constellations.
"Deceive me not my trembling tongue,
Let speech be gone.
The destruction of her painful thoughts
exist in my discorded song."

LOVE LIFE AND FEAR
Romance of a Dreamer

Let me be the dust upon thy trembling
bed where longing blindness fear I sip.
Or on pillows comfort for her heaving breast,
To catch her nightly streams of tenderness.
Let me be her laughter
when laughter lasts beyond the wine,
On heavens gate in equal state we'll fend,
Or doth royalty exists beyond the grave.
Then I'm the voice of the howling wind,
I never cease complaining of cupid's
laughtering grin.
Now lead me to the doorsteps of her dreams,
Protected by her inheritant desire.
Speak oh thunder turning years, speak to her
gently, my undiminishing acquire.

LOVE LIFE AND FEAR
In Search of Self

Who crowneth thou oh opulent,
What fear does your beauty hold?
In face of impenetrable foe, I'll gladly
give my breath.
But with thy beauty,
I am but a whimpering childlike soul.
What takes me back where my infancy was late?
No reply came from the mirror, but in
his glance it bellowed through his ragged state.
Then who gives me songs so faint beyond the grave?
From where doth feelings transcend in search of
mothering faith?
Or am I reincarnated to be depraved?
My soul doth magnify such restless words
that exists like souls in divine purgatory.
I must lay to rest these harnessed feelings,
My place is in her mind, I'm absent in her memory.

THE WINDS OF CHANGE

Newspapers swirl in the face of discontent.
Someone steps on your heels in the grocery line.
In the school yard you hop to my mother's games.
The shapes, they differ but echo just the same.

If the storming airwaves control the wind,
Then let every breath spew lava in it's own face.
Someone bumped your heel with that cart again,
Is he from another place?

Do the mountains still hold hands with the oaks
where they can.
Happiness finds one even in the dark.
Are we shaped like the melting snow
into the form of one,
Where we differ but are not set apart.

Then let all the flowers be of one colour.
What flower will you choose?
And music one note, oh how remote.
Take my palate, but don't taste anger,
Your sight you will loose.
It's the oneness of creation that makes you confused.

FACES

Faces, glowing,
Reflecting the light of the heart.
Don't tap one on the shoulder
to remain in the dark and
through the fog,
Shaded by the anxious breath that
clouds the windows of a home bound train.

You reside in the crystals of the mind,
Where we sip with you again and again
and yet again.

Let the caring endlessness of your reflection
be not for eyes that bring lies.
Loose the hands in the dance around the
fire fueled by exterior beauty only.
They are dancing on the last white cloud
before the midday calamity.

Faces, leaving traces, filling spaces
with kindness.
This beloved mirror of the soul
through the lameness of the eyes,
Your inner beauty we must behold.

Tribute to the land of my birth
from the deepest depths of my heart.

GRENADA

So sweet that gentle breeze from
spicy hills that kisses the morning dew.
Nature's loveliness enshrouds thee,
Soothing the forever in you.

Did your cloud cry in pity
as I departed from thee?
Your noon day message was never lost.
It's the comfort of my dreams
as I frolic through your mountains
with veins of winding streams.

Now like a clown I juggle these lands
which have been good to me.
So very small, why don't I miss you
as you tumble among them before me.

But can one miss the tenderness
of his own soul.
When you are young or growing old.

O Grenada, Grenada,
Your name gives wings to my stride
and my tomorrow
While your blossoming brings pride to
my offspring.
Never shall I capture the stillness of a
setting sun if I should cast but an
unfair shadow upon thee.

THE MYSTERY OF YOUR KISS

When you kiss me, you gently
invite that dozing flower,
The smile within my soul that
waited moment to moment to blossom.
Like the darkened dew that gladly gives
itself to the morning sun.
In my heart another day has begun.

Do I kiss your strength away.
Is that where your mystery fountain
forever flows,
where your love grows. Shhh!

Don't disturb with a word.
A feeling that's already king and
sits on gold,
Basking in a spring of contented desire.

Your kiss removes the mist that
plagues my mind of others.
Its clear so clear, or should I care.
When you're in my world, the world
I do posses bears evenings that transcend
into days,
Not nights. Never loses its light,
Only fades between kisses.
Your kiss is like the completion
of my creation.

RAIN FROM A VIAL

Take a hold of my hand,
You there, foreign man.
Your drifted clouds bring your
conscience to me. Is it pure?
Sparkling moonlight on seashore pure.
Or does it make mothers comforting
breast rip innocence into deformity.

Don't dry my eyes with morsels
while your raindrops kill my streams.
Without my tears I will forget my pain.

Take a hold of my hand.
Are you afraid you will read my palm?
See that forbidden tree planted by thee
where fingers burn and all you ever
learn is how to avoid the flame.
Then should not the harvest be reaped
by the planter? Isn't it his gain?

But you sew and walk away while your
clouds transport the darkness of your vial
into the mouths of infants, so you can gargle
flavours with projections right.
Boys, it was a good year, let us celebrate the night.

THE POETS POEM

In this package like a beach,
Holds your footprints for the next
incoming wave.
No storeroom it contains beneath
the containing sky but swallows
fly to be swallows.

Your soul is slain and lies there by
the waters edge in folded uncertainty.
Music fills the air but not thine.
Happiness is split and christened anew.
Bulging stomach, but hungry eyes
confusion speaks,
"What next do you do?"

Your prints remain circling your direction.
You are on that stage, player or clown.
It's your life I know, but so little do I know.

Within thine own fluttering tongue plays
a guilty heart.
Plug your ears to wisdom,
And dash yourself upon the rock beneath the
blazing lighthouse.

Wisdom will knock but once to the wise
while you lie on ignorant shore
where poems of life exist no more.
To you, the poets die.

AGELESS PROMISES

I reach for your hand
to take me to the other side
to stand in safety's light.

I reach for your dream
that makes me laugh.
'Twas no more in sight.

The stairs I climb in footprints
made for two.
I twinkled in the legacy of you.

Our Christmas Eve sunshine that
that lit the sky,
Now slipped into New Year's uncertainty.

Does growing old grow icicles so cold,
Where kisses had brought sunshine to
bear seems no more there.
Your answering machine said,
"Message please, at the tone."

How many 'I love you's' does it take?
How many 'I love you's' to break that spell
we built so well?
We built that bridge with promises to last,
Hand in hand humbly and poor,
We built that bridge on a golden loop,
And said, "In sickness or in death, forever more."

PRIDE

I am a man, or should I say that I
am a man and son, you are a prince.
Be a prince of pride,
The pride that's so bright it harbors
ambition in its light.

Your teachers, your teachers are the
expectations in your parents eyes
that will prepare your soul for reaping
from life's most fulfilling goal.

Now on this maturing land on which you
stand growing landscapes of towers
your pride is now an armor.
It must protect you from raging tempests
of disdain. Because fools sleep exhaulted
if one allows one's self to be treated
like untied shoe laces in the rain.

Ribbons at the boroughs fair,
Which bloomed into city's sprawling
spiral stairs.
They all splashed in our sweat,
With no regrets, yes with no regrets.

But why, why does my heart wish for
wings each time I have to say to the last
shivering guest who seeks refuge within
this nest,
That I am a man, or should I say that I am a
man and son, you are a prince.
Be a prince of pride.

I'LL SEE YOU PRETTY MAPLE
My Adopted Home, Sweet Canada.

Where first I saw rainbows of men,
Clans and bands from northern territories
to the prairie lands.
Where first I saw cities bursting at its seams,
And customs grow from lands unknown
as from the pages of a dream.

Blessed greatness from shore to shore,
Where tongues will change but still
locked in songs of ancient hills.
And costumes parade among your lakes
colouring your waters still.

My heirs must learn the songs of this land,
Let that river flow into their souls.
Shake hands with its newness
its innocence enriched.
What a country, what a song,
Beauty to behold.

Preserve it, oh Canada as much as you can.
Speak of its beauty in foreign lands.
Seek fortune in gold not buried beneath,
But in rainbow eyes on your street.

Just say good morning, how do you do?
Love thy neighbour one once said.
Bonjour mademoiselle, bonjour.
We both shiver alike, we are the children
of the sap and ten thousand lakes.
We are Canucks.

DOES THE WORLD REVOLVE AROUND YOU

Fearless and bold, gallantly he rode,
Thundering o'er them all
fading like mist beneath his spurs
never yielding to their fall.

Beloved be that one
who mended his soul,
calming life's fury like a dream.
There always there
with loves confident stroke
making a winner out of him.

Peasants dreams,
while sovereign delight materializes
in his grasp.
Ancient cellared wines await his nod,
His parting seems always too fast.

Here he is now with glittering success.
Without her 'twas impossible, oh yes.
His expectations of her, very well met.
Expectations of him!
Oh, not just yet.

A BLACK SANDY BEACH IN PARADISE

Run to the water's edge, taste it's cool,
Ahhh, with your toes.
Walk it's shortening length on it's
misfortune telling lines.
Drawn by meddling waves that
reduces the Sunday soccer field.

Tins of waste and wasted tin cans
tell a nightly tale, of sweetened lies
of defenseless virgins honor, as
we burn sugarcane branches through
the night,
Invented lighthouses to guide our
fathers home.

Nude babies swim before waking
to the bulging eyes of their mothers
and the full moon.

No space for one's feet, it's Sunday.
That's when it's paleness disappears
to frolicking flexing laughter where
only the whiteness of teeth contrast our
blackened sheen.

Have you walked a beach that leaves
enchanting voices in your everywhere,
Where huge stones lurk on the waters
edge like sentries for centuries bearing
names of their very own and dare you find
their look alike anywhere.
Well I know you never walked
my black sandy beach in paradise.

MY FAVOURITE CHAIR

With all fours planted in the shade
of my room,
Saddled like a faithful pony
on the range.
Chest held high, it's majesty and
master to bear,
Invites the winking of my
favorite chair.

My goose bumps quiver in answer
to its call.
Nothing else can soothe me.
Such effortless politeness, I brag
of it all.
It's my coming home, my throne.
It's just a chair, someone once declare.
Oh, is it?

Life's directions I'll receive from my
pulpit true blue.
There, like in purple I'll sit anew.

How can a room hold such comfort
much larger in size,
Where the seasons winds form patterns
with its grains.
The year we fell in love resembled
these moonshaped smiling knots.
Why do I rush to these arms that hold the
secrets of my deepest thoughts.

HAPPINESS

Trembling feet among the crowd,
Falling in despair.
You are there.
Feels like flames that choke the Amazon breeze.
You are there.
Rise, rise go dancing skyward like a kite,
Not anchored by fear.
See dancers seek romance in steps and notes,
Hand in hand to chance.

What measureth happiness and insults your
fathomless soul? Diamonds?
Diamonds that shine on loops of gold
while knees are bent in pledge.
And you wonder how long will those knees
stay bent. Am I wrong?
Then why flicker like candles in the breeze
waiting for a storm?

Echoing laughter transforms you into the light.
Make it your day.
From dust to dawn click your heels like tulips
in the early spring.
Spring to life, you may.

It's you, it's yours, embrace it.
Loose those ha, ha, ha.
Not with arms outstretched grasping moonbeams
in the night, you are my light.
Then light your day, make it stay, just make it stay.

ON THEIR WEDDING DAY

The warmth of your name caresses your presence
at my side.
As we say good night from different places
among such caring faces.
But the night was just another anxious wait
for your voice to unravel the brilliance of my
morning sun.

If life be a bed of roses, let's lie beneath
moistening our kisses with the dew drops
that cascade off its petals to be a part
of this tenderness.

Let wishers wish and hopes be painted
with fading colours of someone else's mind.
Just give me your hand,
Let me touch the stars that will guide me
into my happiness forever.

Today by my side, where angels smile
and knees are bent to respect the One on high.
Our joyous words became a part of what
was already written in our hearts.

Now through the glow of my emotion,
I'm proud to agree once more
that promises will not be promises unless
they begin at our door.
Where happy tears join oceans of well wishers.
For our life, our love, and our devotions.

I TOUCH HEAVEN

No fear shall steal my sleep,
Nor destiny quell the riches of my heart.
I stomp that fire out,
'Twas so great a start.

I claweth not the rolling Earth.
'Tis not meant to hold, but share.
Why clutch the fire of greed,
While in the face of faith stands out a fruitless seed.

Climb the heights where lowliness is aloft.
Angels never rest.
In their toils, whose face do you see,
Redeemed eyes know best.

I hear the groaning earth,
It's thunder clasps closer than a dream.
I see the conquering foes
but not beyond the season's edge.
They wore the crown it seems.

I rest the armor of this world
but found the might that shields beyond belief.
I pity fools that laugh, but fools must laugh for pity
while perishables play games and steal their heart.

Without one dime I purchase myself.
With God, with wisdom and with thought.
I'll see you dear, I'll see you in heaven.

END OF THE CIRCLE

I stride within strides on dust of our dust
as aisles of learning crowns me,
Questioning the wisdom that makes me wise
while I toil with turbulence within me.

All things granted and taken for granted.
I name them all, both animals and trees.
But why, oh why can't I tell when I awake,
Questions I've answered in my dreams?

Like a giant I feel sometimes,
But I fall from the force of a tiny pebble.
In my palms great mysteries unfold
whose magnificence eludes me.
'Cause in my mirror lies my pride
darkening the path before me.

I grasp the word in my flight
and thunder halts outside my door.
Now my heart shines day and night,
I am guaranteed for ever more.
You are guaranteed for ever more
and we are guaranteed for ever more
by the precious blood of the Lamb.

THEN IT RAINED

We were the skylark's starry sky,
With pillowed promises we dance on clouds
as love letters fly
with love winds from our hearts.

Our goodnight kisses bore everlasting
in it's span,
While lovers watch with jealous gaze,
Entrenched in rage. Our depth of love to find.

Your secret eyes stole curiosity.
Drops of your words moistened my growing heart
never to part.
Or should I say severance curse never grew
in spacious contentment we always knew.
We came full circle,
That loop of love around us so bright,
No clouds in sight.

Then it rained.

Those moonlight shadows that drifted unknown
were images of hunters, dwellers of darkness.
As we perched on branches of air,
Wings clutching wings out there.
Another trophy on walls of slanderous tongue
we were made to bear.

THUNDER AND THE MUTE

They applaud your entrance
while you toast in the face of injustice.
Your wants overflow creating a
deafness to my plea.
Your word, always loud with your yesterday's crowd,
Not remembering your existence is me.

Your laughter echoes unfairness
which has become the rhythm of your soul.
You don't step, you are just stumbling into regret.
The truth never sleeps,
Into your life it will creep.
It never dies to riches, or the colour of your eyes.

My voice, just a shadow
it cannot block your path.
But shadows reflect objects,
What's the reflection of your heart?

There is still a voice understood in every language.
It's hoarse from shouting in vain,
So it clears it's throat with the rain.
It speaks for those you consider under.
Prevent the storm.
Listen to the voice of thunder.

GOODBYE TO YOUR MORNING BREW

Parting faces,
Faces that braid in conversations so deep.
Grasping images.
Stop the reign of time tonight,
Go enjoy the moonlight.

Your devotion to this facility that crosses
and criss crosses.
As we say heave ho, on we go,
But who really knows.

We transformed our lives
like walls back to brick
crushing flesh and bones
clearing the way for the unknown.

We are just layers on the shelf,
So let this obligation take it's rest.
Go settle in your feathered nest.
Don't just say this is your time,
Do it your way.

The clouds never did blindfold the sun.
The loss of flight 301 and all 189 persons
in the waters of the Dominican Republic.

CRIMSON CRYSTALS

The sun was bright as a gift of day.
The welcoming sky invited them to stay.
As faces gleamed with protective sheen
they toasted the end of their holiday.

Where did such tragedy conceal itself in
luggage no heavier in weight.
But weight that weight that weighed beneath the waves
to toll solemn church bells on the river Rhine.

Fortunes she traded, it was her gift.
A gift it was meant to be,
And she blamed her soul in faithlessness,
The hidden darkness of such tragedy.

The babe within her was the first bearer of the news.
On her knees she stayed 'til dawn.
She listened for that crushing heel,
The final chapter of her song.

She asked that unforgettable soul
who cursed his tongue for message so lame,
"Should I clear a space on the banks for two,
Or play their favorite music to ease
my unborn's pain?"

THE VILLAGE GATE

"Sing my name, yea birds among those hills.
My voice has lost its footing."
Now I taste the salt that withers
I am home to stay for the longest evening.

I heave my muted words in clearing
patches in the dark,
As the viewing time expired,
I ran them wild like players in the park,
Feelings not yet unfurled.

Must I steal the sparrow's songs as
he entices his mate.
My words lay heavy like on a liars tongue.
My strength I'll place upon those hills,
Mingled with my forefathers abound.

I stood and shouted my name,
No echoes in my voice.
"I'm home! I'm home! I'm home!"
No one came running.
The runners passed with glee.
I had to search the empty eyes of those
I thought should remembered me.

Should I return to that land
that first glowed beyond your jagged clouds.
Now night has come and seasons weigh late,
I lay my soul to rest at the village gate.